TABLE OF CONTENTS

Disclaimer -   2
About the Author -   3-4
Introduction -   5-7
- Why You Need a Revocable Trust Now
- What This Book Will Teach You
- Why Act Now?

Chapter 1: What Is a Revocable Trust? The Foundation of Estate Planning   8-11
- What Is a Revocable Trust?
- Key Components of a Revocable Trust
- Why a Revocable Trust?
- Debunking Common Myths About Revocable Trusts
- Real-Life Examples
- Why Start Now?

Chapter 2: Revocable Trusts vs. Wills: Understanding the Differences -   12-17
- The Basics of a Will
- What Sets a Revocable Trust Apart
- Side-by-Side Comparison
- Common Misconceptions About Wills and Trusts
- Why Avoid Probate?
- Real-Life Scenarios
- Choosing What's Right for You

Chapter 3: Avoiding Probate: Why a Trust Saves Time and Money -   18-22
- What Is Probate?
- How a Revocable Trust Avoids Probate
- The Hidden Costs of Probate
- Time Is Another Cost
- Privacy Matters
- Real-Life Examples

Chapter 4: Control and Flexibility: How Revocable Trusts Work During Your Lifetime -   23-28

- Maintaining Control
- Adapting to Life's Changes
- Planning for Incapacity
- Controlling Asset Distribution
- Real-Life Example: The Flexible Trust

Chapter 5: Privacy Matters: Keeping Your Estate Out of Public Records - 29-34
- The Public Nature of Probate
- How a Revocable Trust Protects Your Privacy
- Case Study: The Importance of Privacy
- Maintaining Privacy During Incapacity
- Privacy in a Digital Age

Chapter 6: Protecting Your Family from Disputes and Legal Challenges - 35-40
- The Risk of Family Disputes
- How a Revocable Trust Prevents Disputes
- Real-Life Examples
- Additional Features That Prevent Disputes
- Protecting Vulnerable Beneficiaries

Chapter 7: Planning for Incapacity - 41-46
- The Challenges of Incapacity Without a Trust
- How a Revocable Trust Addresses Incapacity
- Coordinating Your Trust with Other Legal Tools
- Real-Life Examples
- The Emotional Benefits of Planning Ahead

Chapter 8: Funding Your Trust: Transferring Assets for Maximum Protection -
47-52
- Why Funding Your Trust Is Crucial
- The Asset Transfer Process
- Common Mistakes to Avoid
- Funding a Trust for Digital Assets
- Real-Life Examples

Chapter 9: Revocable Trusts for Blended Families -   53-58
- The Challenges of Estate Planning for Blended Families
- How a Revocable Trust Can Help
- Key Strategies for Blended Families
- Real-Life Examples
- Common Pitfalls to Avoid

Chapter 10: Providing for Minors and Special Needs Beneficiaries -   59-64
- Why Wills Alone Are Not Enough
- Using a Trust for Minors
- Special Needs Beneficiaries
- Real-Life Examples
- The Emotional Benefits

Chapter 11: Tax Efficiency: The Financial Benefits of Revocable Trusts -   65-70
- Understanding Tax Implications
- Types of Taxes to Consider
- How a Revocable Trust Supports Tax Efficiency
- Combining with Other Tax-Saving Tools
- Real-Life Examples

Chapter 12: Avoiding Common Pitfalls -   71-77
- Common Mistakes and Solutions
- Real-Life Examples
- Key Steps to Success
- The Cost of Poor Planning

Chapter 13: Updating Your Revocable Trust -   78-83
- The Importance of Regular Updates
- When to Update Your Trust
- How to Update Your Trust
- Best Practices
- Real-Life Examples

Chapter 14: The Role of a Trustee -   84-90

- What Does a Trustee Do?
- Qualities of an Effective Trustee
- Types of Trustees
- How to Choose the Right Trustee
- Real-Life Examples

Chapter 15: Taking the First Step: How to Create a Revocable Trust Today -

91-96

- Define Your Goals
- Hire an Estate Planning Attorney
- Draft the Trust Document
- Fund the Trust
- Communicate Your Plan
- Real-Life Example

Appendix: Planning Your Revocable Trust -   97-101
- Comprehensive Estate Planning Questionnaire
- Personal Information
- Family Information
- Financial Information
- Distribution Preferences
- Special Instructions

DISCLAIMER

This book, **"Securing Your Family's Future: Why You Need a Revocable Trust Now,"** is intended for informational and educational purposes only. It does not constitute legal advice or create an attorney-client relationship between the reader and the author. Every individual's circumstances are unique, and estate planning decisions should be made in consultation with a qualified attorney or legal professional who can provide advice tailored to your specific needs and local laws.

The author and publisher disclaim all liability for any actions taken or not taken based on the information contained in this book. For personalized legal guidance, please seek the assistance of a licensed attorney in your jurisdiction.

About the Author

Mario M. Blanch, Esq. is a seasoned attorney and the founding partner of **Blanch Legal Firm**, based in West New York, New Jersey. With decades of legal experience in estate planning, family law, and litigation, Mr. Blanch is dedicated to helping families secure their futures through practical and compassionate legal guidance.

Born in New York City and raised in North Bergen, New Jersey, Mr. Blanch has a deep connection to the communities he serves. He earned his degree in Economics from Rutgers University and his Juris Doctorate from Seton Hall University School of Law, where he developed a passion for justice and equitable representation. Early in his career, Mr. Blanch clerked for the Honorable Marguerite T. Simon in the Bergen County Chancery Division, where he gained expertise in probate, trust administration, and complex legal disputes. This foundation laid the groundwork for his dedication to estate planning and protecting families during life's most challenging transitions.

As the founder of **Blanch Legal Firm**, Mr. Blanch has worked tirelessly to provide clients with tailored solutions to their legal needs, including creating revocable trusts that help families avoid probate, reduce conflict, and ensure seamless transitions of wealth. He has handled thousands of cases, including real estate transactions, trust disputes, and family law matters, with a focus on securing outcomes that align with his clients' values and long-term goals. His experience in both litigation and planning gives him a unique perspective on how to design estate plans that work in real life, not just on paper.

Mr. Blanch's approach to estate planning is rooted in his belief that everyone deserves peace of mind, regardless of their financial circumstances. Fluent in Spanish, he works to make legal services accessible to diverse communities, offering compassionate advice and clear solutions. Whether helping families navigate complex blended family dynamics, plan for special needs beneficiaries, or protect their assets from unnecessary legal battles, Mr. Blanch is committed to empowering his clients to make informed decisions.

In **"Securing Your Family's Future: Why You Need a Revocable Trust Now,"** Mr. Blanch combines his extensive legal knowledge with his dedication to client care. This book reflects his passion for educating families about the importance of proactive estate planning and the transformative power of a well-structured revocable trust.

Mario M. Blanch's mission is simple: to provide families with the tools and guidance they need to protect their loved ones, preserve their legacies, and find peace of mind in an uncertain world.

Introduction

Planning for the future is one of the most important acts of love and responsibility you can offer your family. Yet, many people put off estate planning, thinking it's unnecessary, overly complicated, or something only the wealthy need. Unfortunately, waiting too long—or failing to plan altogether—can leave your loved ones facing significant legal, financial, and emotional challenges. The truth is, estate planning isn't just about dividing assets; it's about protecting your family, ensuring your wishes are honored, and creating a legacy of security and stability.

At the heart of a successful estate plan lies one of the most powerful and versatile tools available: the **revocable trust**. This legal structure goes beyond the limitations of a will, offering flexibility, control, and peace of mind. A revocable trust allows you to manage your assets during your lifetime, plan for potential incapacity, and ensure a smooth and private transfer of wealth to your beneficiaries after your passing.

Why You Need a Revocable Trust Now

Many people mistakenly believe that estate planning can wait until retirement or that a simple will is sufficient to protect their family. However, life is unpredictable, and unforeseen events—such as illness, injury, or death—can happen at any time. Without a comprehensive plan in place, your family could face:

1. **Lengthy and Costly Probate:**

    - A will must go through probate, a court-supervised process that can take months or even years to complete. Probate fees, attorney costs, and delays can significantly erode the value of your estate.

2. **Unnecessary Taxes and Expenses:**

    - Without proper planning, your estate could be subject to avoidable taxes, reducing what your loved ones inherit.

3. **Family Disputes:**

- Ambiguities in your estate plan or the lack of a clear plan altogether can lead to conflicts, legal challenges, and strained relationships among your heirs.

4. **Public Exposure:**

    - Probate is a public process, meaning details about your assets, debts, and beneficiaries are accessible to anyone.

A revocable trust addresses these challenges by bypassing probate, providing privacy, and offering flexibility to adapt to life's changes. Whether your estate is simple or complex, a revocable trust ensures that your family is protected from unnecessary stress and uncertainty.

What This Book Will Teach You

This book, "Securing Your Family's Future: Why You Need a Revocable Trust Now," is your comprehensive guide to understanding and implementing a revocable trust as the cornerstone of your estate plan. You'll learn:

- **How a Revocable Trust Works:** Understand the basics of trusts, their benefits, and how they differ from wills.
- **Avoiding Probate and Legal Challenges:** Discover how a trust simplifies the estate settlement process and protects your family from unnecessary delays and expenses.
- **Planning for Incapacity:** Learn how a trust ensures your assets are managed and your wishes are respected if you become unable to make decisions.
- **Caring for Loved Ones:** Explore strategies for providing for minor children, special needs beneficiaries, and blended families.
- **Tax Efficiency:** Understand how a trust integrates with other tools to minimize taxes and preserve more of your wealth for future generations.
- **Choosing the Right Trustee:** Get guidance on selecting the best person or entity to manage your trust.

Each chapter is designed to demystify the estate planning process, offering practical advice and real-life examples to help you make informed decisions.

Why Act Now?

The best time to create a revocable trust is today. Waiting until "the right time" often leads to missed opportunities and leaves your family vulnerable to unnecessary complications. Estate planning isn't about wealth—it's about protecting your loved ones and ensuring your values and priorities are honored.

This book is a call to action. By taking the time to understand and establish a revocable trust, you're making an investment in your family's security and peace of mind. Let's embark on this journey together and create a plan that protects what matters most to you.

Welcome to **"Securing Your Family's Future."** It's time to take the first step toward a brighter, more secure tomorrow.

Chapter 1: What Is a Revocable Trust? The Foundation of Estate Planning

Estate planning can feel overwhelming, especially when faced with the myriad of tools and terms that come with it. Among the most powerful and flexible tools available is the **revocable trust**. Sometimes referred to as a **living trust**, this legal entity forms the foundation of a secure and effective estate plan. Whether you are new to estate planning or looking to refine your strategy, understanding the purpose and benefits of a revocable trust is a vital first step.

What Is a Revocable Trust?

A **revocable trust** is a legal arrangement where you (the grantor) transfer ownership of your assets into the trust during your lifetime. You retain control over these assets as the trustee, and you can change, modify, or revoke the trust at any time—hence the term "revocable."

Unlike a will, which only takes effect after your death, a revocable trust operates during your lifetime and can continue seamlessly if you become incapacitated. Upon your passing, the trust's provisions dictate how your assets are distributed to your beneficiaries, without the need for probate.

Key Components of a Revocable Trust

To better understand how a revocable trust works, let's break down its essential elements:

1. **The Grantor (You):**

   - The person who creates the trust and transfers assets into it.
   - Retains full control over the trust during their lifetime.

2. **The Trustee (Initially You):**

   - The individual or entity responsible for managing the trust's assets.
   - You can name yourself as the initial trustee and appoint a successor trustee to step in upon your incapacity or death.

3. **The Successor Trustee:**

    - The person or entity who takes over the management of the trust when the original trustee is no longer able to serve.
    - This is a crucial role and must be filled by someone you trust implicitly.

4. **The Beneficiaries:**

    - The individuals or organizations who will receive the trust's assets after your death.
    - Beneficiaries can include family members, friends, or charitable organizations.

5. **The Trust Document:**

    - The legal document that establishes the trust, outlining its terms, the roles of the trustee and successor trustee, and the distribution of assets.

Why a Revocable Trust?

A revocable trust provides solutions to several challenges inherent in traditional estate planning. Here's why it's often considered the backbone of a modern estate plan:

1. **Control During Your Lifetime:**

    - You maintain full control of the assets within the trust.
    - You can sell, buy, or modify assets as you would if they were in your name.

2. **Avoiding Probate:**

    - Probate is the court-supervised process of distributing your estate after death. It can be time-consuming, expensive, and public.
    - Assets in a revocable trust bypass probate entirely, providing a quicker, private, and less costly way to distribute your assets.

3. **Incapacity Planning:**

    o If you become incapacitated due to illness or injury, your successor trustee can step in to manage your assets without requiring court intervention.
    o This ensures continuity and avoids the need for a court-appointed guardian.

4. **Flexibility:**

    o Life circumstances change. A revocable trust allows you to update beneficiaries, add or remove assets, and even revoke the trust entirely.

5. **Privacy:**

    o Unlike wills, which become public during probate, a trust remains private.
    o This confidentiality protects your family from scrutiny and potential disputes.

Debunking Common Myths About Revocable Trusts

There are several misconceptions about revocable trusts that often deter people from using this essential tool. Let's clear up the most common ones:

- **"I don't have enough assets to need a trust."**
  Trusts aren't just for the wealthy. A trust can protect your home, savings, investments, and even personal belongings, regardless of your net worth.

- **"I'm too young to worry about estate planning."**
  Estate planning isn't about age—it's about readiness. Unforeseen circumstances can happen to anyone, making it vital to plan early.

- **"My spouse or children will automatically inherit everything."**
  Without a trust, your estate will go through probate, where distribution may not align with your wishes. A trust ensures your assets are distributed

exactly as you intend.

- **"Trusts are too complicated and expensive."**
  While creating a trust involves an initial investment of time and money, the long-term benefits far outweigh these costs. It simplifies the estate management process, saving your family stress and expense later.

Real-Life Examples

To illustrate the importance of revocable trusts, let's consider two hypothetical families:

1. **The Johnsons:**
   The Johnsons had a will but no trust. When Mr. Johnson passed away, the family's assets went through probate. The process took 18 months, cost the family thousands in court and attorney fees, and exposed personal details about their estate.

2. **The Parkers:**
   The Parkers established a revocable trust. When Mrs. Parker became incapacitated, her successor trustee seamlessly took over asset management, avoiding court intervention. After her death, the assets were distributed to the beneficiaries within weeks—privately and without probate.

Why Start Now?

A revocable trust is not something to leave until later in life. The earlier you establish your trust, the sooner you can ensure your family is protected from unnecessary legal battles, delays, and stress.

Takeaways from This Chapter:

- A revocable trust gives you control, flexibility, and peace of mind.
- It avoids the delays, costs, and publicity of probate.
- It ensures a seamless transition in the event of incapacity or death.

This is your opportunity to take charge of your estate and protect your family's future. As you'll learn in the upcoming chapters, a revocable trust is not just a tool for the wealthy—it's a practical solution for anyone who values control, privacy, and efficiency in their estate plan.

Chapter 2: Revocable Trusts vs. Wills: Understanding the Differences

When it comes to estate planning, two primary tools are often compared: the **revocable trust** and the **will**. Both serve essential purposes, but they function differently and have distinct advantages and limitations. Understanding these differences is key to determining why a revocable trust might be the better choice for you and your family.

The Basics of a Will

A **will**, or last will and testament, is a legal document that specifies how your assets should be distributed after your death. It also allows you to name an executor to oversee the distribution process and appoint guardians for minor children.

While a will is a foundational estate planning document, it has several limitations:

1. **Requires Probate:**

   - Probate is the court-supervised process of validating a will and distributing assets to heirs. It can be time-consuming, expensive, and public.

2. **Limited to Post-Death Planning:**

   - A will takes effect only after you die. It does not address scenarios where you become incapacitated and cannot manage your assets.

3. **Public Record:**

   - Once a will is filed for probate, it becomes a matter of public record. This lack of privacy can expose sensitive family and financial information.

What Sets a Revocable Trust Apart

A **revocable trust** goes beyond the limitations of a will by providing a more comprehensive approach to managing and distributing your assets. Here's how it differs:

1. **Avoids Probate:**

    - Assets held in a trust bypass the probate process, allowing for a faster, more private, and less costly transfer to beneficiaries.

2. **Incapacity Planning:**

    - A trust includes provisions for managing your assets if you become incapacitated, ensuring your finances and property are handled according to your wishes.

3. **Privacy:**

    - A trust remains private, protecting your estate from public scrutiny and shielding your beneficiaries from potential disputes or challenges.

4. **Immediate Effect:**

    - A trust takes effect as soon as it's created, enabling you to manage your assets during your lifetime while providing for their distribution upon your death.

Side-by-Side Comparison

Feature	Will	Revocable Trust
Takes Effect	After death	During lifetime
Incapacity Planning	No	Yes
Avoids Probate	No	Yes

Privacy	No (Public)	Yes (Private)
Cost to Create	Lower upfront costs	Higher upfront costs
Control During Lifetime	Limited	Full control
Time to Distribute Assets	Months or years (due to probate)	Weeks or months (no probate)

Common Misconceptions About Wills and Trusts

1. **"My Will Can Do Everything a Trust Does."**
    - While a will specifies who inherits your property, it does not avoid probate or provide for incapacity planning. A trust is more versatile and comprehensive.
2. **"Only the Wealthy Need Trusts."**
    - Trusts are often associated with large estates, but they are practical for anyone who values privacy, efficiency, and avoiding probate.
3. **"Trusts Are Too Complicated."**
    - While trusts require careful planning, they simplify estate management for your loved ones and reduce legal complications after your passing.

Why Avoid Probate?

Probate is a major consideration when deciding between a will and a trust. While some people assume probate is straightforward, it often comes with significant drawbacks:

1. **Time:**

   - Probate can take months or even years, delaying asset distribution.
   - This can create financial strain for heirs who may need immediate access to funds.

2. **Cost:**

   - Court fees, attorney fees, and executor commissions can consume a substantial portion of your estate.
   - Costs typically range from 3% to 7% of the estate's total value.

3. **Public Nature:**

   - Probate proceedings are public, meaning anyone can access details about your estate, beneficiaries, and financial situation.

4. **Family Disputes:**

   - Probate often invites disputes among family members, especially if the will's terms are unclear or contested.

The Best of Both Worlds

For most people, a combination of a will and a revocable trust is the ideal solution. While the trust handles most of the estate, the will acts as a safety net for assets not placed in the trust. This is often referred to as a **pour-over will**, which ensures that any assets inadvertently left out of the trust are "poured over" into it upon your death.

Real-Life Scenarios

Scenario 1: Using a Will Alone

- *Jane, a widow with two children, relied solely on her will to distribute her assets.*
- After her death, her estate entered probate, which lasted over 18 months and incurred significant legal fees. Her children faced delays in accessing their inheritance and had to attend multiple court hearings.

Scenario 2: Using a Revocable Trust

- *Mark created a revocable trust and transferred all his assets into it.*
- When he passed away, his successor trustee immediately distributed the assets according to his wishes, bypassing probate entirely. The process was quick, private, and cost-effective, sparing his family unnecessary stress.

Choosing What's Right for You

While a will is an essential part of any estate plan, it cannot match the flexibility, efficiency, and privacy of a revocable trust. By combining both tools, you can ensure that every aspect of your estate is covered, providing peace of mind for you and your loved ones.

Key Takeaways:

1. A revocable trust offers significant advantages over a will, including avoiding probate, planning for incapacity, and maintaining privacy.
2. While a will is necessary, it should complement—not replace—a trust in a comprehensive estate plan.
3. Probate can be costly, time-consuming, and public, making a trust the preferred option for many families.

By choosing a revocable trust, you are taking a proactive step toward securing your family's future, ensuring they are protected from unnecessary delays, expenses, and conflicts.

Chapter 3: Avoiding Probate: Why a Trust Saves Time and Money

One of the most compelling reasons to establish a **revocable trust** is its ability to bypass probate. Probate is often misunderstood as a simple legal formality, but in reality, it can be a lengthy, expensive, and invasive process. For families grieving the loss of a loved one, the additional burden of probate can create unnecessary stress and hardship. A revocable trust eliminates this burden, offering a streamlined and private way to distribute your assets.

What Is Probate?

Probate is the legal process through which a deceased person's will is validated, debts are settled, and assets are distributed to heirs. If there is no will, the court follows state intestacy laws to determine how the estate is divided. While probate serves an important function, it is often fraught with complications:

1. **Court Supervision:**
    - The court oversees the distribution of assets, adding layers of bureaucracy.
2. **Time-Consuming:**
    - Probate can take months or even years to complete, delaying access to funds and property.
3. **Costly:**
    - Court fees, attorney fees, and executor commissions can consume a significant portion of the estate.
4. **Public Process:**
    - Probate proceedings are a matter of public record, exposing sensitive details about your assets and beneficiaries.

How a Revocable Trust Avoids Probate

When assets are placed into a **revocable trust**, they are no longer considered part of your probate estate. Instead, they are governed by the terms of the trust, which allows them to pass directly to your beneficiaries upon your death. This process is faster, more efficient, and completely private.

1. **Immediate Transfer of Assets:**

    o Upon your death, the successor trustee assumes control and begins distributing assets according to your instructions.

2. **No Court Involvement:**

    o The court has no role in overseeing the distribution, eliminating delays and reducing legal fees.

3. **Simplified Process:**

    o Beneficiaries receive their inheritance quickly and without the complications of probate.

The Hidden Costs of Probate

Many people underestimate the financial and emotional toll of probate. While specific costs vary by state, probate often involves:

1. **Court Fees:**

    o Filing fees can range from a few hundred to several thousand dollars, depending on the size of the estate.

2. **Attorney Fees:**

    o Attorneys typically charge a percentage of the estate's value or bill hourly, which can add up quickly.

3. **Executor Fees:**

    o Executors are entitled to compensation, which is often a percentage of the estate's value.

4. **Appraisal Costs:**

    - Real estate, jewelry, and other valuable assets must be appraised to determine their worth, adding another layer of expense.

Example:
For an estate worth $500,000, probate fees could easily total $25,000 to $50,000. This money comes directly out of the estate, reducing the inheritance left for your beneficiaries.

Time Is Another Cost

Even a straightforward probate process can take six months to a year, while more complex cases may stretch on for years. During this time:

- Beneficiaries may be unable to access funds needed for living expenses or emergencies.
- Family members may need to attend court hearings, adding stress to an already emotional situation.
- Disputes among heirs may arise, further delaying the process.

Privacy Matters

Probate records are public, meaning anyone can access information about your estate, including:

- The value of your assets.
- The names of your beneficiaries.
- Family conflicts or legal disputes.

For many families, this lack of privacy can lead to unwanted scrutiny, solicitations, or even fraud.

Real-Life Examples

Scenario 1: The Probate Nightmare

When Emily passed away, she left behind a will naming her three children as equal heirs to her estate, which included her home, savings, and personal belongings. Since her assets were not held in a trust, the estate had to go through probate. The process lasted 18 months, during which the children couldn't sell the house or access the funds they needed. Legal and court fees consumed 6% of the estate's value, reducing their inheritance.

Scenario 2: The Seamless Transition

In contrast, David created a revocable trust and transferred all his assets into it before his death. When he passed, his successor trustee immediately began distributing the assets according to the trust's terms. The process took a few weeks, and there were no court fees or delays. David's family was spared the stress and cost of probate.

The Emotional Toll

The probate process can exacerbate family tensions, especially when:

- Heirs disagree over the distribution of assets.
- Debts or taxes reduce the estate's value, leaving less to divide.
- The process drags on for years, creating uncertainty and frustration.

By avoiding probate, a revocable trust spares your loved ones from these challenges, allowing them to focus on healing and moving forward.

Funding the Trust

To ensure your trust avoids probate, it's essential to **fund** it correctly. This means transferring ownership of your assets—such as real estate, bank accounts, and investments—into the trust. Any assets left outside the trust may still be subject to probate.

Why Revocable Trusts Are Essential

While avoiding probate is just one benefit of a revocable trust, it is often the most immediate and impactful. By bypassing this cumbersome process, you:

- Save your family time, money, and stress.
- Ensure your assets are distributed quickly and privately.
- Protect your loved ones from the uncertainties of court proceedings.

Key Takeaways from This Chapter

1. Probate is a costly, time-consuming, and public process that can significantly reduce the value of your estate.
2. A revocable trust allows your assets to bypass probate, providing a faster, more private, and cost-effective solution.
3. Properly funding your trust is essential to ensure it achieves its intended purpose.

By creating a revocable trust, you are taking a proactive step to protect your family's financial future and emotional well-being. This simple yet powerful tool offers peace of mind and ensures that your loved ones are spared unnecessary hardship.

Chapter 4: Control and Flexibility: How Revocable Trusts Work

During Your Lifetime

One of the greatest advantages of a **revocable trust** is the control and flexibility it offers during your lifetime. Unlike other estate planning tools, a revocable trust isn't just for the future—it's a living document that can be used to manage your assets right now. Whether you want to make adjustments to your plan, protect your finances in case of incapacity, or simplify how your estate is distributed after your passing, a revocable trust gives you the power to adapt to life's changes.

Maintaining Control

When you create a revocable trust, you are the **grantor**, and in most cases, you will also serve as the initial **trustee**. This means that even though your assets are legally held by the trust, you retain complete control over them.

- **You decide how the assets are managed.**
- **You can buy, sell, or modify the assets in the trust at any time.**
- **You can amend or revoke the trust entirely.**

This control ensures that a revocable trust doesn't feel like a restrictive or permanent decision. Instead, it functions as an extension of your personal management of your finances.

Adapting to Life's Changes

Life rarely stays the same. From getting married to having children, starting a business, or going through a divorce, your financial and personal circumstances can shift dramatically over time. A revocable trust offers the flexibility to adapt to these changes seamlessly.

Common Life Events That May Require Trust Updates:

1. **Marriage or Divorce:**

- Add or remove a spouse as a beneficiary.
- Update provisions to reflect your new marital status.

2. **Birth or Adoption of a Child:**

    - Include new children or grandchildren as beneficiaries.
    - Establish specific provisions for their care and financial support.

3. **Significant Financial Changes:**

    - Add newly acquired assets to the trust.
    - Adjust how assets are distributed based on changes in your financial situation.

4. **Death of a Beneficiary or Trustee:**

    - Update your trust to remove or replace individuals who are no longer able to serve in their designated roles.

5. **Relocation to a New State or Country:**

    - Revocable trusts are generally valid across state lines, but certain state laws may require updates to ensure full compliance.

6. **Charitable Goals:**

    - Add or modify charitable beneficiaries if your philanthropic priorities change.

Planning for Incapacity

One of the most practical benefits of a revocable trust is its ability to protect you and your assets in the event of incapacity. While many people think of estate planning as something that only applies after death, incapacity planning is just as critical.

How a Trust Works in Case of Incapacity:

1. **Successor Trustee:**

   - When you create a trust, you name a successor trustee who will step in to manage your assets if you are unable to do so.
   - This avoids the need for a court-appointed guardian or conservator.

2. **Seamless Transition:**

   - Unlike other arrangements that require legal intervention, a trust allows for a smooth and immediate transition of control.

3. **Financial Protection:**

   - Your successor trustee will use the assets in the trust to cover your medical bills, daily expenses, and other financial obligations according to your instructions.

4. **Maintaining Privacy:**

   - Court-appointed guardianship proceedings are often public, exposing personal and financial details. A trust keeps these matters private.

Example:

Imagine you experience a medical emergency that leaves you unable to manage your finances. With a revocable trust in place, your successor trustee can immediately step in to pay bills, oversee investments, and handle other responsibilities—all without court involvement. This ensures your affairs are managed according to your wishes, sparing your family from difficult decisions.

Controlling Asset Distribution

A revocable trust gives you the ability to distribute your assets exactly as you see fit. This control extends beyond simply deciding who receives what; it allows you to include detailed instructions and conditions for how and when distributions are made.

Customizable Distribution Options:

1. **Staggered Distributions:**

    o Instead of providing a lump sum, you can distribute assets in stages—e.g., when a beneficiary reaches a certain age or milestone (such as graduating college).

2. **Specific Purposes:**

    o You can allocate funds for specific purposes, such as education, medical expenses, or the purchase of a home.

3. **Protecting Vulnerable Beneficiaries:**

    o If a beneficiary struggles with financial management, you can set up provisions to protect their inheritance from being misused or claimed by creditors.

4. **Special Needs Trusts:**

    o For beneficiaries with disabilities, you can create a special needs trust within the revocable trust to ensure they receive support without jeopardizing government benefits.

Example:

You may want to leave money to your grandchildren but prefer they not have access to the funds until they turn 25. A revocable trust allows you to establish this condition, ensuring the inheritance is used wisely.

Simplifying Estate Management

One of the main reasons people choose a revocable trust is to simplify the management of their estate. Unlike a will, which requires court oversight through probate, a trust allows your assets to be managed and distributed without judicial involvement.

How It Simplifies Your Estate:

- Assets are immediately accessible to the trustee, eliminating delays.

- Beneficiaries receive their inheritance without the costs or complications of probate.
- The process is private, keeping family affairs out of public records.

Real-Life Example: The Flexible Trust

The Case of Sarah and James:
Sarah and James, a married couple in their 40s, created a revocable trust to ensure their two children would be cared for in case of an emergency. Over the years, they made updates to the trust:

- When they had a third child, they added her as a beneficiary.
- When James started a business, they included the business assets in the trust.
- After Sarah's father passed away, they inherited property, which they transferred to the trust.

When James was diagnosed with a degenerative illness, Sarah stepped in as the successor trustee, managing the trust's assets seamlessly. This allowed her to focus on James's care without the burden of court involvement.

Key Takeaways

1. A revocable trust allows you to retain control over your assets while providing the flexibility to adapt to life's changes.
2. It protects your financial interests in case of incapacity, ensuring your assets are managed according to your wishes.
3. You can customize asset distribution to meet the unique needs of your beneficiaries.
4. A revocable trust simplifies estate management, sparing your loved ones from the complexities of probate.

By establishing a revocable trust, you are taking proactive steps to secure not only your family's future but also your financial stability during your lifetime. The flexibility and control offered by a trust make it one of the most valuable tools in estate planning.

Chapter 5: Privacy Matters: Keeping Your Estate Out of Public Records

Privacy is a cornerstone of estate planning, yet many people overlook how important it is to keep their financial and personal matters confidential. Without proper planning, the details of your estate, including the value of your assets, the names of your beneficiaries, and the specifics of your final wishes, can become part of the public record through the probate process.

A **revocable trust** solves this problem by allowing you to transfer assets to your heirs privately, bypassing probate and keeping your affairs out of public view. For those who value discretion and wish to protect their loved ones from unnecessary scrutiny, a trust is an indispensable tool.

The Public Nature of Probate

Probate is not just time-consuming and expensive—it's also a public process. When a will is submitted to the court for validation, it becomes part of the court's public records, accessible to anyone who wishes to review it.

What Becomes Public During Probate?

1. **Your Assets:**

   - The court documents will list the assets in your estate, including property, bank accounts, investments, and personal belongings.
   - The total value of your estate is also disclosed.

2. **Your Beneficiaries:**

   - The names of those inheriting your assets, along with the specifics of what they receive, become public knowledge.

3. **Family Disputes:**

   - If your will is contested, the details of the legal battle—including sensitive family dynamics—can become part of the public record.

This lack of privacy can expose your family to:

- **Solicitations:** Scammers and unethical individuals may target beneficiaries, especially those receiving large inheritances.
- **Family Strife:** Public knowledge of who inherits what can lead to jealousy or disputes among family members.
- **Safety Concerns:** Disclosure of assets, such as valuable collections or properties, may increase the risk of theft or fraud.

How a Revocable Trust Protects Your Privacy

When you use a revocable trust, your estate bypasses probate entirely. The trust operates outside the court system, meaning there is no public record of its contents or distributions.

Key Privacy Benefits of a Revocable Trust:

1. **Confidential Asset Distribution:**
   - Only the trustee and beneficiaries are privy to the terms of the trust and the details of the asset distribution.
   - No outsiders, including creditors or the general public, have access to this information.
2. **No Public Record:**
   - The trust document is not filed with the court, keeping your financial matters private.
3. **Shielding Family Matters:**
   - Sensitive family situations, such as unequal distributions or provisions for estranged relatives, remain confidential.

Case Study: The Importance of Privacy

Scenario 1: Public Probate Process

John passed away, leaving behind a will that divided his $3 million estate among his three children. Since his estate had to go through probate, court documents revealed the value of his estate and the details of the distributions. Soon after, John's youngest child, who received the largest share, was inundated with phone calls from financial advisors, charities, and even scammers offering "investment opportunities."

Scenario 2: Private Trust Administration

Maria, in contrast, established a revocable trust that held her assets. When she passed away, her successor trustee distributed the assets privately, in accordance with Maria's instructions. No court filing was necessary, and the family's financial matters remained confidential. This privacy protected Maria's beneficiaries from external pressures and preserved their peace of mind.

Maintaining Privacy During Incapacity

Privacy isn't just important after death; it's also critical during your lifetime. If you become incapacitated without a trust, a court may appoint a guardian or conservator to manage your financial affairs. These proceedings are public, potentially exposing details about your health and finances.

With a revocable trust, your successor trustee takes over asset management without court involvement, ensuring that your privacy is preserved even during periods of incapacity.

Privacy in a Digital Age

The digital era has heightened concerns about privacy, making a revocable trust even more valuable. Today, information spreads quickly, and public probate records can be easily accessed or shared online. A trust shields your estate from these vulnerabilities, providing an added layer of protection for your family.

Blended Families and Privacy

Privacy can be particularly important for blended families, where estate plans may involve children from previous marriages, new spouses, or other complex dynamics. A trust allows you to make personalized decisions without exposing these arrangements to public scrutiny, reducing the risk of tension or conflict among family members.

Key Steps to Maximize Privacy

To ensure your estate plan achieves the level of privacy you desire, follow these best practices:

1. **Fund Your Trust Properly:**
   - Transferring assets into the trust is crucial. Any assets left outside the trust may still be subject to probate, negating the privacy benefits.
2. **Work with an Attorney:**
   - A qualified estate planning attorney can help you structure your trust to minimize public exposure and meet your specific privacy goals.
3. **Include Digital Assets in Your Plan:**
   - Incorporate instructions for managing online accounts, cryptocurrencies, and other digital assets to ensure a seamless and private transition.
4. **Update Your Trust Regularly:**
   - Life changes, such as new assets or beneficiaries, may require updates to your trust. Keeping it current ensures that your privacy and estate planning goals are maintained.

Why Privacy Matters

Many people underestimate the value of privacy in estate planning. While it's easy to focus on financial efficiency or tax savings, privacy is equally important in protecting your family's well-being. By choosing a revocable trust, you're not just securing your assets—you're also shielding your loved ones from unnecessary exposure, stress, and risk.

Key Takeaways

1. Probate is a public process that exposes your financial and personal affairs to public scrutiny.
2. A revocable trust bypasses probate, keeping the details of your estate confidential.
3. Privacy protects your family from unwanted attention, disputes, and potential fraud.
4. Properly funding and updating your trust ensures that your privacy goals are fully realized.

By establishing a revocable trust, you are taking a critical step to safeguard your legacy and protect your family from the prying eyes of the public. Privacy isn't just a luxury—it's an essential part of securing your family's future.

Chapter 6: Protecting Your Family from Disputes and Legal Challenges

When it comes to inheritance, even the most close-knit families can face disagreements. Without a clear and enforceable estate plan, disputes over assets, guardianship, or perceived inequalities can escalate into legal battles. These conflicts not only drain financial resources but also fracture relationships, leaving lasting scars.

A **revocable trust** significantly reduces the risk of disputes by providing clear, legally binding instructions for the management and distribution of your assets. This chapter explores how trusts protect your family from unnecessary conflicts and ensure your wishes are carried out smoothly.

The Risk of Family Disputes

Families are complex, and emotions often run high when dealing with the death of a loved one. Even in situations where there is no apparent conflict, certain scenarios can lead to disputes, including:

1. **Ambiguities in a Will:**

    - Vague or unclear language in a will can lead to differing interpretations, sparking disagreements.

2. **Perceived Favoritism:**

    - Unequal distributions or perceived favoritism among beneficiaries can create resentment and tension.

3. **Blended Families:**

    - Conflicts often arise when children from previous marriages feel their interests are overshadowed by the surviving spouse or step-siblings.

4. **Unexpected Beneficiaries:**

    - Leaving assets to a charity, friend, or distant relative can surprise family members and lead to challenges.

5. **Probate Delays:**

    o The lengthy probate process can amplify stress and create opportunities for disputes.

How a Revocable Trust Prevents Disputes

A revocable trust provides clarity and legal certainty, reducing the chances of disagreements among your heirs. Here's how:

1. Clear Instructions

- A trust allows you to spell out exactly how your assets should be distributed, leaving no room for ambiguity.
- You can include detailed provisions, such as:
    - o Setting conditions for distributions.
    - o Addressing specific needs of individual beneficiaries.

2. Avoiding Probate

- Probate is a common source of family disputes, as it brings your estate under court supervision and invites legal challenges.
- A trust bypasses probate entirely, ensuring that your wishes are carried out privately and efficiently.

3. Naming a Trustee

- By appointing a trustee (or successor trustee), you designate a neutral party to manage and distribute assets according to your instructions.
- If conflicts arise, the trustee has the authority to resolve them based on the trust's terms, reducing the likelihood of court involvement.

4. Flexibility for Complex Families

- In blended families, trusts allow you to balance the interests of your current spouse with those of children from previous marriages.

- You can create tailored provisions to ensure everyone's needs are met without creating friction.

5. Protection from Challenges

- While wills are more susceptible to legal challenges, trusts are harder to contest.
- The private nature of a trust reduces opportunities for disputes to arise in the first place.

Real-Life Example: Avoiding Disputes

Scenario 1: Conflict Over a Will

When Linda passed away, her will left most of her estate to her second husband, with only a modest sum allocated to her children from her first marriage. Feeling slighted, her children challenged the will in court, arguing that Linda had been coerced into changing her estate plan. The legal battle dragged on for years, draining the estate's resources and permanently damaging family relationships.

Scenario 2: Clarity with a Trust

In contrast, Tom created a revocable trust to divide his estate between his second wife and his children from his first marriage. The trust outlined specific distributions and included provisions for his wife to remain in the family home while ensuring his children received their inheritance. Tom's clear instructions eliminated ambiguity, and his successor trustee administered the trust smoothly, avoiding conflicts.

Additional Features That Prevent Disputes

1. **Staggered or Conditional Distributions:**
   - To prevent misuse of funds or disputes over large lump sums, a trust can stagger distributions over time or include conditions, such as reaching a certain age or completing an educational milestone.

2. **Trustee Discretion:**
    - You can grant your trustee discretion to make decisions about discretionary distributions, such as additional support for a beneficiary facing financial hardship.
3. **No-Contest Clauses:**
    - A no-contest clause can discourage beneficiaries from challenging the trust by disinheriting anyone who attempts to do so.

Protecting Vulnerable Beneficiaries

Certain beneficiaries may need extra protection to ensure their inheritance is managed responsibly. A revocable trust allows you to address these concerns:

1. **Minors:**
    - A trust can hold assets for minor children until they reach an age you consider appropriate for them to manage their inheritance.
2. **Special Needs Beneficiaries:**
    - You can create a special needs trust within the revocable trust to provide for a disabled beneficiary without jeopardizing their eligibility for government benefits.
3. **Beneficiaries with Financial Challenges:**
    - If a beneficiary struggles with debt or poor financial decisions, the trust can limit their access to funds or provide for professional management of their inheritance.

Minimizing the Role of the Court

By creating a revocable trust, you reduce the need for court involvement in the management and distribution of your estate. This:

- Speeds up the process of transferring assets.
- Lowers the cost of administering your estate.
- Minimizes the opportunity for disputes to escalate into costly litigation.

Selecting the Right Trustee

The trustee plays a critical role in preventing disputes. Choose someone who is:

- Trustworthy and impartial.
- Financially responsible and detail-oriented.
- Willing and able to handle the administrative duties of the trust.

If no suitable individual is available, consider appointing a professional trustee, such as a bank or trust company.

Key Takeaways

1. A revocable trust minimizes the risk of family disputes by providing clear, legally binding instructions for asset distribution.
2. Avoiding probate eliminates one of the main sources of legal challenges and family conflict.
3. Trusts offer tailored solutions for blended families, minors, special needs beneficiaries, and others with unique needs.
4. Appointing the right trustee ensures that your wishes are carried out efficiently and without bias.

By establishing a revocable trust, you are not just planning for the future—you are protecting your family from the stress, cost, and emotional toll of legal disputes. In doing so, you preserve harmony and ensure that your legacy is honored as you intended.

Chapter 7: Planning for Incapacity: The Role of Revocable Trusts in Healthcare and Finances

Life is unpredictable, and while many people focus on planning for what happens after they're gone, planning for **incapacity** is just as important. Incapacity—whether due to illness, injury, or cognitive decline—can leave you unable to manage your finances or make critical decisions about your healthcare. Without a plan in place, your loved ones may face significant legal, financial, and emotional challenges as they scramble to fill the gap.

A **revocable trust** serves as a powerful tool to prepare for these scenarios. It allows you to plan for the management of your assets and ensure your wishes are respected, even if you are no longer able to advocate for yourself.

The Challenges of Incapacity Without a Trust

If you become incapacitated without a revocable trust or other legal arrangements, your family may need to petition the court to appoint a **guardian** or **conservator** to manage your affairs. This process is not only time-consuming and expensive but also emotionally taxing for your loved ones.

Common Problems Families Face:

1. **Court Involvement:**
   - Guardianship proceedings can take weeks or months, leaving your finances unmanaged during the interim.
   - The court may appoint someone to manage your affairs who does not fully understand or prioritize your wishes.
2. **Family Conflicts:**
   - Disputes often arise over who should serve as the guardian or conservator.
   - These conflicts can create lasting divisions among family members.

3. **Public Exposure:**

    o Guardianship proceedings are public, exposing private details about your health and finances.
4. **Unintended Decisions:**

    o Without clear instructions, your guardian or conservator may make decisions that don't align with your values or priorities.

How a Revocable Trust Addresses Incapacity

A **revocable trust** allows you to name a **successor trustee** who can step in to manage your assets if you become incapacitated. This eliminates the need for court intervention and ensures that your finances are handled according to your instructions.

Key Features of a Trust for Incapacity Planning:

1. **Successor Trustee Provisions:**

    o When creating your trust, you designate a successor trustee who will take over in the event of your incapacity.

    o This individual or entity is legally bound to follow the terms of the trust.
2. **Immediate Access to Assets:**

    o The successor trustee can immediately access the trust's assets to pay bills, manage investments, and cover medical expenses.
3. **Customized Instructions:**

    o You can include specific guidelines in the trust for how your assets should be managed during your incapacity.
4. **Avoiding Court Intervention:**

- By eliminating the need for a court-appointed guardian or conservator, you reduce delays, costs, and potential conflicts.

Coordinating Your Trust with Other Legal Tools

While a revocable trust plays a central role in incapacity planning, it works best when integrated with other estate planning documents, such as:

1. Durable Power of Attorney:

- A durable power of attorney allows you to appoint someone to handle financial matters that are not covered by the trust, such as filing taxes or accessing retirement accounts.

2. Healthcare Proxy or Advance Directive:

- These documents designate someone to make medical decisions on your behalf if you cannot do so.
- They can be used alongside your trust to ensure your overall plan reflects your wishes.

3. HIPAA Authorization:

- A HIPAA authorization allows your trustee or healthcare proxy to access your medical records, ensuring they have the information needed to make informed decisions.

Real-Life Example: Incapacity Planning in Action

Scenario 1: Without a Trust

Mike, a retired teacher, suffered a debilitating stroke that left him unable to manage his finances. His adult children were forced to petition the court for guardianship, a process that took six months and cost thousands of dollars in legal fees. In the meantime, bills went unpaid, his investments were neglected, and family members argued over who should be in charge.

Scenario 2: With a Trust

In contrast, Susan, a small business owner, had established a revocable trust and named her sister as the successor trustee. When Susan was diagnosed with Alzheimer's, her sister immediately stepped in to manage the trust's assets, ensuring that Susan's bills were paid, her investments were managed, and her care needs were funded—all without court involvement.

Choosing the Right Successor Trustee

Selecting the right person or entity to serve as your successor trustee is one of the most important decisions you'll make when creating a trust.

Qualities to Look For:

1. **Trustworthiness:**

    o The trustee must have integrity and a strong sense of responsibility.

2. **Financial Competence:**

    o They should be capable of managing investments, paying bills, and handling other financial tasks.

3. **Availability:**

    o The trustee must be willing and able to dedicate the time required to manage your affairs.

4. **Impartiality:**

    o A neutral party may be the best choice if family dynamics are complex.

Professional Trustees:

If no suitable individual is available, consider naming a professional trustee, such as a bank or trust company. While this option involves fees, professional trustees bring expertise and objectivity to the role.

Avoiding Pitfalls in Incapacity Planning

To ensure your plan works as intended, follow these best practices:

1. **Update Your Trust Regularly:**
    - Review your trust periodically to ensure it reflects your current financial situation and family dynamics.
2. **Communicate Your Plan:**
    - Inform your successor trustee and key family members about your plan to avoid surprises and misunderstandings.
3. **Include Specific Instructions:**
    - Clearly outline your wishes for managing your assets during incapacity to minimize guesswork.
4. **Coordinate with Other Documents:**
    - Ensure your trust aligns with your power of attorney, healthcare proxy, and other legal tools for a cohesive plan.

The Emotional Benefits of Planning Ahead

Incapacity planning isn't just about managing finances—it's about relieving your loved ones of the burden of making difficult decisions without guidance. By creating a revocable trust, you:

- Protect your family from the stress of court proceedings.
- Provide clarity and direction, reducing the risk of conflict.
- Ensure that your wishes are respected, even when you cannot advocate for yourself.

Key Takeaways

1. Incapacity can happen to anyone, making proactive planning essential.
2. A revocable trust eliminates the need for court-appointed guardianship, providing a seamless transition of asset management.
3. Naming a trusted successor trustee ensures your finances are handled responsibly during your incapacity.
4. Combining a trust with other tools, like a power of attorney and healthcare proxy, creates a comprehensive plan for your care and financial well-being.

By planning for incapacity now, you protect yourself and your loved ones from uncertainty and hardship. A revocable trust not only secures your assets but also ensures that your legacy reflects your values, even during life's most challenging moments.

Chapter 8: Funding Your Trust: Transferring Assets for Maximum Protection

Creating a **revocable trust** is only the first step in securing your family's future. For the trust to fulfill its purpose, it must be properly funded. Funding a trust means transferring ownership of your assets into the trust, ensuring they are governed by its terms and can avoid probate. Without funding, the trust is little more than an empty shell—legally valid but practically ineffective.

In this chapter, we'll explore the process of funding your trust, common mistakes to avoid, and how to ensure all your assets are properly accounted for.

Why Funding Your Trust Is Crucial

A revocable trust only applies to assets that are placed under its ownership. If assets are not transferred into the trust, they will not bypass probate and may be distributed according to a will (if one exists) or state intestacy laws (if no will is present). This can lead to:

1. **Probate Exposure:**
   - Assets left outside the trust may still need to go through probate, undermining the trust's purpose.
2. **Confusion Among Beneficiaries:**
   - If some assets are governed by the trust while others are subject to a will or intestacy laws, conflicts may arise among heirs.
3. **Missed Tax Benefits:**
   - Certain assets may lose tax advantages if not properly transferred to the trust.

The Asset Transfer Process

Step 1: Inventory Your Assets

Begin by making a comprehensive list of all your assets, including:

- Real estate.
- Bank accounts (checking, savings, CDs).
- Investment accounts (stocks, bonds, mutual funds).
- Retirement accounts (401(k)s, IRAs).
- Life insurance policies.
- Business interests.
- Personal property (jewelry, vehicles, collectibles).

Step 2: Determine Which Assets to Transfer

While many assets can and should be placed in your trust, some may be better left out or require special handling:

Assets to Transfer:

1. **Real Estate:**
   - Transferring real estate into a trust ensures it avoids probate. This includes primary residences, vacation homes, and investment properties.
2. **Bank Accounts:**
   - Most checking, savings, and money market accounts can be retitled in the name of the trust.
3. **Investments:**
   - Stocks, bonds, and brokerage accounts should be transferred to the trust to ensure smooth management and distribution.
4. **Business Interests:**

- If you own a business, transferring ownership or your share of the business into the trust can provide continuity.
5. **Titled Personal Property:**
    - Vehicles, boats, and other titled assets can often be transferred to the trust, though local DMV rules may vary.

Assets to Handle Differently:

1. **Retirement Accounts (401(k), IRA):**
    - These accounts are typically not transferred into a trust due to tax implications. Instead, name the trust as a contingent or secondary beneficiary.
2. **Life Insurance Policies:**
    - You can name the trust as the beneficiary of your life insurance policy to direct proceeds according to the trust's terms.
3. **Health Savings Accounts (HSAs):**
    - Like retirement accounts, HSAs are usually left in your name, with the trust named as a beneficiary.

Step 3: Retitle Assets

For the trust to own an asset, its title must reflect the trust's name. This process varies depending on the type of asset:

Real Estate:

- Execute a new deed transferring ownership to the trust. For example, a property titled to "John Doe" would be retitled to "John Doe, Trustee of the Doe Family Revocable Trust."
- Ensure the deed is properly recorded with the local county recorder's office.

Bank and Investment Accounts:

- Contact your financial institution and request the necessary forms to retitle accounts.
- Provide a copy of the trust document, if required.

Vehicles:

- Check your state's DMV rules for transferring ownership of vehicles to a trust.

Business Interests:

- Review your business's operating agreement or bylaws to determine how ownership can be transferred to the trust.
- Update business records to reflect the trust's ownership.

Common Mistakes to Avoid

1. Forgetting to Fund the Trust

One of the most common mistakes is creating a trust but failing to transfer assets into it. An unfunded trust provides no probate protection and leaves your estate vulnerable to legal complications.

2. Not Updating Beneficiary Designations

For retirement accounts, life insurance, and similar assets, failing to name the trust as a beneficiary can result in unintended distributions.

3. Leaving Out Newly Acquired Assets

Assets acquired after the trust's creation must also be transferred into the trust. Many people forget to update their trust after buying new property, opening new accounts, or inheriting assets.

4. Overlooking Small or Forgotten Assets

Items like safety deposit boxes, digital assets, and smaller personal belongings are often overlooked but can create legal complications if not properly accounted for.

Funding a Trust for Digital Assets

In today's digital world, many people hold valuable assets online, such as:

- Cryptocurrencies.
- Digital wallets.
- Social media accounts.
- Online businesses or domains.

These assets can also be included in your trust. Create a list of all digital assets, along with login information, and include instructions for their management and transfer within the trust.

Updating and Maintaining Your Trust

Funding your trust is not a one-time process. To ensure your trust remains effective:

1. **Review It Regularly:**
   - Schedule periodic reviews of your trust to confirm all assets are properly accounted for.
2. **Update It After Major Life Events:**
   - Marriage, divorce, births, deaths, or significant financial changes may require adjustments to your trust.
3. **Communicate with Your Trustee:**
   - Keep your successor trustee informed about the trust's contents and any changes you make.

Real-Life Example: Proper Funding in Action

Scenario 1: An Unfunded Trust

John spent considerable time and money creating a comprehensive revocable trust, but he forgot to transfer his home and savings accounts into it. When he passed away, his family discovered that these assets had to go through probate, negating the trust's main benefits.

Scenario 2: A Fully Funded Trust

Emily not only created a trust but also worked diligently to transfer all her assets into it, including her home, investments, and digital assets. Upon her death, her successor trustee was able to distribute the assets quickly and privately, avoiding probate and family disputes.

Key Takeaways

1. Funding a trust is essential for it to work as intended. Without proper funding, assets may still go through probate.
2. Retitle key assets like real estate, bank accounts, and investments to the trust's name.
3. Handle retirement accounts and life insurance differently by naming the trust as a beneficiary.
4. Regularly review and update your trust to account for new assets and life changes.
5. Include digital assets and ensure all instructions are clear for your trustee.

By taking the time to properly fund your trust, you maximize its benefits and ensure your estate is protected. This step transforms your trust from a legal document into a powerful tool for securing your family's future.

Chapter 9: Revocable Trusts for Blended Families / Ensuring Fair Distribution

Blended families—those that include children from previous marriages, new spouses, or stepchildren—face unique challenges in estate planning. Balancing the interests of various family members while maintaining harmony requires careful thought and clear instructions. Without proper planning, misunderstandings and disputes can arise, potentially leading to fractured relationships or legal battles.

A **revocable trust** is a powerful tool for blended families, offering flexibility, clarity, and control to ensure that your estate is distributed fairly and according to your wishes. This chapter focuses on the strategies you can use to protect your loved ones while addressing the complexities of a blended family dynamic.

The Challenges of Estate Planning for Blended Families

Blended families bring unique dynamics that can complicate estate planning. Common challenges include:

1. Competing Interests:

- A surviving spouse may have different priorities than children from a previous marriage.
- Children from different relationships may have conflicting expectations about inheritance.

2. Unequal Distributions:

- Providing for a surviving spouse while ensuring children from a prior marriage are not left out can be difficult to balance.

3. Potential Conflicts:

- Tensions may arise if beneficiaries feel the estate plan is unfair or favors one party over another.

4. Unintended Disinheritance:

- Without proper planning, a surviving spouse could unintentionally exclude children from a previous marriage, or vice versa.

How a Revocable Trust Can Help

A revocable trust provides the structure and flexibility needed to address these challenges while protecting your family's financial future.

1. Customized Asset Distribution:

- You can specify exactly how your assets will be distributed, ensuring that both your spouse and children are provided for.

Example:

- You might allocate a portion of your assets to your spouse for their lifetime use, with the remainder passing to your children upon your spouse's death.

2. Avoiding Probate:

- A trust bypasses probate, ensuring that your estate is distributed quickly and privately. This reduces the risk of disputes and keeps family matters out of the public record.

3. Protecting Your Spouse and Children:

- Trust provisions can ensure your surviving spouse has access to necessary resources while safeguarding a portion of your estate for your children.

4. Reducing the Risk of Legal Challenges:

- A trust is harder to contest than a will, providing an added layer of protection against disputes.

Key Strategies for Blended Families

1. Establish a Qualified Terminable Interest Property (QTIP) Trust:

- A QTIP trust allows you to provide income and support for your surviving spouse while preserving the trust's principal for your children or other beneficiaries.
- This strategy ensures your spouse is cared for without jeopardizing your children's inheritance.

2. Create Separate Trusts for Each Party:

- For complex situations, you may create separate trusts for your spouse and children. This ensures clear boundaries and reduces the potential for conflict.

Example:

- One trust could hold assets for your spouse's use, while another distributes assets directly to your children from a prior marriage.

3. Staggered or Conditional Distributions:

- To prevent a single lump-sum payout that might be misused or create jealousy, you can stagger distributions over time or include conditions, such as reaching a certain age or milestone.

4. Appoint an Impartial Trustee:

- In blended families, appointing a neutral or professional trustee can reduce tension and ensure that the trust is administered fairly.

5. Address Stepchildren Clearly:

- If you wish to include or exclude stepchildren, specify your intentions in the trust to avoid ambiguity and potential disputes.

Real-Life Examples: Planning for Blended Families

Scenario 1: No Plan in Place

David remarried and had two children from his first marriage. He died unexpectedly without an estate plan. Under state intestacy laws, his entire estate passed to his new wife, leaving his children from the previous marriage with nothing. This caused resentment and strained relationships between the surviving spouse and David's children.

Scenario 2: Using a Revocable Trust

Sarah, also in a blended family, established a revocable trust that specified her husband would receive income from her investments for the rest of his life. Upon his death, the remaining principal would be distributed equally among her children from her first marriage. This arrangement ensured that all parties were cared for, reducing the risk of disputes.

Communicating Your Plan

Transparency is key in blended families. While it may be uncomfortable, discussing your estate plan with your spouse and children can:

1. Clarify your intentions.
2. Reduce misunderstandings.
3. Prevent surprises after your passing.

Updating Your Trust

Blended family dynamics often change over time. Regularly review and update your trust to account for:

- Changes in family relationships.
- The birth of new children or grandchildren.
- Divorce or remarriage.
- Significant changes in your financial situation.

Common Pitfalls to Avoid

1. Overlooking the Needs of One Party:

- Ensure your plan balances the needs of your spouse and children to prevent conflict.

2. Failing to Specify Terms Clearly:

- Ambiguous instructions can lead to disputes and challenges.

3. Neglecting Stepchildren:

- If you wish to include stepchildren as beneficiaries, make this explicit in your trust.

4. Not Consulting an Attorney:

- Blended family situations can be complex. A qualified estate planning attorney can help you navigate these challenges.

Key Takeaways

1. Blended families face unique estate planning challenges, including competing interests and potential conflicts.
2. A revocable trust provides flexibility and clarity, ensuring that your spouse and children are cared for according to your wishes.
3. Strategies like QTIP trusts, staggered distributions, and appointing an impartial trustee can help reduce disputes.
4. Regularly update your trust to reflect changes in family dynamics or financial circumstances.
5. Open communication with your loved ones can prevent misunderstandings and foster harmony.

By using a revocable trust to plan for your blended family, you can achieve a fair and balanced distribution of your assets while preserving family relationships.

Your trust becomes more than a legal tool—it becomes a blueprint for peace and security in the years to come.

Chapter 10: Providing for Minors and Special Needs Beneficiaries with a Trust

When planning your estate, it's crucial to consider the unique needs of minors and beneficiaries with disabilities. Children and individuals with special needs often require additional protection and thoughtful planning to ensure their well-being. A **revocable trust** offers the flexibility and control needed to address these concerns, providing a secure foundation for their future while avoiding potential complications.

In this chapter, we'll explore strategies for using a revocable trust to care for minors and special needs beneficiaries, from setting conditions for distributions to establishing specialized trusts.

Why Wills Alone Are Not Enough

While a will can name guardians and dictate how assets should be distributed, it lacks the flexibility and protection of a trust.

Limitations of a Will for Minors:

1. **Guardianship Requirements:**
    - A will can name a guardian, but the court must approve the appointment.
2. **Probate Delays:**
    - Assets distributed through a will must go through probate, delaying access.
3. **Lack of Asset Management:**
    - Minors cannot legally manage inherited assets, often leading to court-appointed conservators.

Challenges for Special Needs Beneficiaries:

1. **Impact on Government Benefits:**

- Direct inheritance through a will can disqualify a beneficiary from needs-based programs like Medicaid or Supplemental Security Income (SSI).
2. **Lack of Oversight:**
    - Without a trust, funds may be mismanaged or spent irresponsibly.

A revocable trust addresses these issues, providing clear, enforceable instructions for managing and distributing assets.

Using a Trust for Minors

Minors cannot legally manage property or make financial decisions, so assets left to them must be managed by an adult or entity. A revocable trust allows you to designate a trustee to oversee the inheritance and ensures that the funds are used appropriately.

Key Features for Minors:

1. **Naming a Trustee:**

    - The trustee manages the assets on behalf of the minor until they reach the age specified in the trust.
2. **Setting Conditions for Distribution:**

    - You can specify how and when assets are distributed. For example:
        - **Staggered Distributions:** Release funds at milestones such as age 18, 25, or 30.
        - **Purpose-Driven Distributions:** Allocate funds for education, medical expenses, or other specific needs.
3. **Avoiding Court Intervention:**

    - Unlike a will, a trust avoids the need for court-appointed guardians or conservators, reducing delays and legal fees.
4. **Providing Oversight:**

- The trustee ensures that the assets are used responsibly until the beneficiary is capable of managing them independently.

Special Needs Beneficiaries: Protecting Eligibility for Benefits

Individuals with disabilities may rely on government programs like Medicaid or SSI to cover medical care, housing, and daily living expenses. Receiving an inheritance outright could disqualify them from these benefits.

A **special needs trust** within a revocable trust allows you to provide for a beneficiary without jeopardizing their eligibility for government assistance.

How a Special Needs Trust Works:

1. **Preserving Benefits:**
    - Assets in a special needs trust are not counted as income for Medicaid or SSI eligibility.
    - The trust provides supplemental funds to enhance the beneficiary's quality of life without replacing government benefits.
2. **Flexible Support:**
    - The trust can cover non-essential expenses such as:
        - Medical treatments not covered by insurance.
        - Educational programs.
        - Travel and entertainment.
3. **Trustee Management:**
    - The trustee manages the trust's funds, ensuring they are used in accordance with government regulations and the grantor's wishes.

Choosing the Right Trustee

The trustee plays a vital role in ensuring that minors and special needs beneficiaries receive the support they need.

Qualities to Look For:

1. **Trustworthiness:**
   - The trustee must act in the best interests of the beneficiary.
2. **Financial Expertise:**
   - Managing investments, paying expenses, and complying with legal requirements requires a level of financial acumen.
3. **Patience and Understanding:**
   - Beneficiaries, especially those with special needs, may require extra care and attention.

Professional Trustees:

If no suitable individual is available, consider appointing a professional trustee, such as a bank or trust company, to manage the trust.

Real-Life Examples

Case 1: A Trust for a Minor

Scenario: Emily passed away, leaving behind a 12-year-old son, Alex.
Without a Trust:

- Alex's inheritance was tied up in probate, and the court appointed a conservator to manage the funds until Alex turned 18. Upon reaching adulthood, Alex received a lump sum, which he spent irresponsibly within a year.

With a Trust:

- Emily created a revocable trust, naming her sister as the trustee. The trust provided funds for Alex's education and living expenses and staggered the remaining distributions at ages 21 and 30. This structure ensured long-term financial support and stability.

Case 2: A Special Needs Trust

Scenario: Mark wanted to leave an inheritance for his daughter, Lisa, who has autism and relies on Medicaid for her care.

Without a Trust:

- Mark's will left Lisa $250,000, disqualifying her from government benefits until the funds were depleted.

With a Trust:

- Mark established a special needs trust within his revocable trust. The funds were used to enhance Lisa's quality of life—covering therapy, recreation, and travel—while preserving her eligibility for Medicaid and SSI.

Avoiding Common Pitfalls

1. **Forgetting to Update the Trust:**

    - Regularly review your trust to account for changes in your beneficiaries' circumstances.

2. **Neglecting to Fund the Trust:**

    - Ensure all assets intended for minors or special needs beneficiaries are transferred into the trust.

3. **Choosing the Wrong Trustee:**

    - Appoint a trustee who is capable, impartial, and willing to fulfill their duties over the long term.

4. **Failing to Use a Special Needs Trust:**

- Direct inheritances for special needs beneficiaries can have unintended consequences. Always consult an estate planning attorney to structure the trust correctly.

The Emotional Benefits

Planning for minors and special needs beneficiaries goes beyond financial considerations—it provides peace of mind. Knowing that your loved ones will be cared for in a manner that reflects your values and priorities can alleviate much of the stress associated with estate planning.

Key Takeaways

1. A revocable trust ensures minors receive their inheritance in a structured and responsible manner, avoiding court intervention.
2. Special needs trusts protect eligibility for government benefits while enhancing the beneficiary's quality of life.
3. Choosing the right trustee is critical to ensuring proper management and care for vulnerable beneficiaries.
4. Regularly updating your trust ensures it continues to meet the needs of your family as circumstances change.

By incorporating provisions for minors and special needs beneficiaries into your revocable trust, you create a lasting legacy of care, stability, and security for the people who matter most.

Chapter 11: Tax Efficiency: The Financial Benefits of Revocable Trusts

When it comes to estate planning, minimizing taxes is a critical consideration. While a **revocable trust** is not primarily designed to reduce taxes, it can play an integral role in a larger strategy for tax efficiency. By working in tandem with other estate planning tools, a revocable trust helps ensure that your assets are preserved for your beneficiaries, rather than being consumed by unnecessary tax burdens or expenses.

In this chapter, we'll explore how revocable trusts can contribute to tax efficiency and provide practical strategies for integrating them into your estate plan.

Understanding the Tax Implications of Revocable Trusts

A revocable trust, by its nature, does not directly reduce taxes during your lifetime or at your death. Because the trust is revocable, you maintain control of the assets within it, and they are still considered part of your taxable estate. However, the trust can be a critical component of a tax-efficient estate plan by:

1. **Streamlining Administration:**

    - Bypassing probate reduces administrative costs and associated taxes, preserving more of your estate for beneficiaries.

2. **Facilitating Tax Strategies:**

    - Trusts can be structured to work alongside other tax-saving mechanisms, such as irrevocable trusts, gifting strategies, or charitable donations.

Types of Taxes to Consider

1. Estate Taxes

- Federal estate taxes apply to estates exceeding a certain threshold ($12.92 million in 2023, subject to change).
- Some states impose their own estate taxes, often with much lower thresholds.

2. Inheritance Taxes

- Inheritance taxes are levied on beneficiaries, depending on their relationship to the deceased and state laws.

3. Income Taxes

- Income generated by assets in the trust is typically taxed as personal income during your lifetime. After your death, income taxes may apply to your estate or beneficiaries.

How a Revocable Trust Supports Tax Efficiency

1. Avoiding Probate Costs

While probate taxes are not the same as federal estate taxes, probate often involves fees tied to the size of your estate. By placing assets in a revocable trust, you bypass probate entirely, saving thousands in administrative costs and fees.

Example:

- Without a trust, a $1 million estate might incur probate fees of 2-4%, totaling $20,000 to $40,000. A revocable trust eliminates this cost.

2. Leveraging Portability of the Estate Tax Exemption

For married couples, a revocable trust can facilitate the portability of the federal estate tax exemption. This means that if one spouse dies without using their full exemption, the unused portion can be transferred to the surviving spouse, doubling the amount shielded from estate taxes.

Strategy:

- Include provisions in your trust to maximize portability, ensuring your family benefits from the full exemption.

3. Simplifying Gifting Strategies

A revocable trust can help you implement a gifting strategy to reduce the size of your taxable estate. By transferring assets into the trust and making annual gifts to beneficiaries (up to the annual gift tax exclusion amount, currently $17,000 per recipient in 2023), you can reduce the overall value of your estate while providing for your loved ones during your lifetime.

Combining a Revocable Trust with Other Tax-Saving Tools

A revocable trust works best when paired with additional estate planning strategies designed to minimize taxes.

1. Irrevocable Trusts

While a revocable trust does not directly reduce estate taxes, an irrevocable trust can. Assets transferred to an irrevocable trust are no longer considered part of your taxable estate, which can reduce or eliminate estate tax liability.

Example:

- Use a revocable trust to manage your day-to-day finances and an irrevocable trust to hold high-value assets, such as life insurance policies or investment accounts.

2. Charitable Trusts

A charitable remainder trust (CRT) or charitable lead trust (CLT) can work alongside your revocable trust to reduce estate taxes while supporting your philanthropic goals.

- **Charitable Remainder Trust:** Provides income to your beneficiaries during their lifetime, with the remainder going to charity.
- **Charitable Lead Trust:** Pays income to a charity for a set period, with the remainder passing to your beneficiaries.

3. Generation-Skipping Transfer (GST) Trusts

A GST trust allows you to pass assets directly to grandchildren or future generations, bypassing estate taxes for one generation. Your revocable trust can complement this strategy by providing funds or managing assets for the GST trust.

4. Qualified Terminable Interest Property (QTIP) Trusts

For married couples, a QTIP trust can provide income to the surviving spouse while preserving the principal for other beneficiaries, such as children from a prior marriage. A revocable trust can act as a funding mechanism for the QTIP trust.

Planning for State-Specific Taxes

In addition to federal estate taxes, many states impose their own taxes on estates and inheritances. Some states have much lower thresholds for taxation, which can catch families by surprise.

Strategies for State Taxes:

1. Use a revocable trust to transfer assets to beneficiaries located in states without inheritance taxes.
2. Consider relocating high-value assets to states with more favorable tax laws.
3. Work with an estate planning attorney familiar with state-specific rules to optimize your trust for tax efficiency.

Real-Life Examples

Case 1: Using a Revocable Trust to Avoid Probate Costs

Tom's estate was worth $2 million, primarily consisting of real estate and investment accounts. By transferring his assets into a revocable trust, he avoided probate fees of approximately $60,000 and ensured that his beneficiaries received their inheritance without unnecessary delays or expenses.

Case 2: Combining Trusts for Tax Savings

Martha had a $10 million estate and wanted to minimize her tax liability while supporting her favorite charity. She used a revocable trust for her primary assets and created a charitable remainder trust to donate $2 million to a local nonprofit. This strategy reduced her taxable estate while supporting a cause she cared about.

Common Mistakes to Avoid

1. Relying Solely on a Revocable Trust for Tax Savings

- A revocable trust is not a substitute for tax-specific strategies like irrevocable trusts or gifting plans.

2. Failing to Address State Taxes

- Neglecting state-specific rules can result in unexpected tax burdens for your beneficiaries.

3. Not Updating Your Trust

- Tax laws change frequently. Failing to update your trust to reflect current laws can lead to missed opportunities for savings.

Key Takeaways

1. A revocable trust itself does not reduce taxes but can be a cornerstone of a broader tax-efficient estate plan.
2. Combining a revocable trust with other tools, such as irrevocable trusts, charitable trusts, or gifting strategies, can significantly reduce tax liability.

3. Avoiding probate with a revocable trust preserves more of your estate for your beneficiaries.
4. Regularly review and update your trust to account for changes in tax laws and financial circumstances.

By using a revocable trust to complement tax-saving strategies, you protect your family's inheritance while ensuring that your estate plan aligns with your financial goals. This proactive approach secures your legacy and provides peace of mind for the future.

Chapter 12: Avoiding Common Pitfalls: Mistakes to Avoid When Creating a Trust

Establishing a **revocable trust** is one of the most effective ways to secure your family's future, but even the best plans can go awry if critical steps are overlooked. From failing to properly fund the trust to appointing the wrong trustee, seemingly small missteps can lead to costly consequences, leaving your loved ones unprotected.

In this chapter, we'll explore the most common mistakes people make when creating a trust and provide actionable tips to avoid them. By understanding these pitfalls, you can ensure your trust works as intended and delivers the protection and benefits your family deserves.

Mistake 1: Failing to Fund the Trust

A revocable trust is only effective if it is funded. Funding the trust involves transferring ownership of your assets into the trust or designating the trust as a beneficiary. Unfortunately, many people create a trust but fail to take this critical step, leaving their assets exposed to probate.

How to Avoid This Mistake:

1. **Conduct a Comprehensive Asset Review:**

    - Identify all assets you wish to place in the trust, including real estate, bank accounts, investments, and personal property.

2. **Transfer Ownership:**

    - Work with your attorney or financial institution to retitle assets in the name of the trust.

3. **Designate Beneficiaries:**

    - For accounts like retirement plans and life insurance, name the trust as a beneficiary when appropriate.

Mistake 2: Choosing the Wrong Trustee

The trustee plays a vital role in managing the trust and ensuring your wishes are carried out. Selecting someone who is unqualified, uninterested, or biased can lead to mismanagement, delays, or even legal disputes.

How to Avoid This Mistake:

1. **Evaluate the Candidate's Qualifications:**

   - Choose someone who is financially responsible, trustworthy, and capable of handling administrative tasks.

2. **Consider a Professional Trustee:**

   - If family dynamics are complex or you lack a suitable individual, a professional trustee, such as a bank or trust company, can provide impartial and expert management.

3. **Name a Backup Trustee:**

   - Designate a successor trustee to step in if the primary trustee is unable or unwilling to serve.

Mistake 3: Neglecting to Update the Trust

Life changes—such as marriage, divorce, the birth of a child, or the acquisition of new assets—can render your trust outdated. Failing to update your trust regularly can lead to unintended consequences, such as disinheriting a new spouse or excluding a recently born grandchild.

How to Avoid This Mistake:

1. **Schedule Regular Reviews:**

   - Review your trust every 3–5 years or after significant life events.

2. **Communicate with Your Attorney:**
   - Work with an estate planning attorney to ensure updates are legally sound and reflect your current intentions.
3. **Keep a List of Changes:**
   - Maintain a record of any assets or beneficiaries added or removed from the trust to ensure nothing is overlooked.

Mistake 4: Using Ambiguous Language

Unclear or vague instructions in your trust can lead to confusion, misinterpretation, and disputes among beneficiaries.

How to Avoid This Mistake:

1. **Be Specific:**
   - Clearly outline how assets should be distributed, including any conditions or restrictions.
2. **Include Contingency Plans:**
   - Specify what should happen if a primary beneficiary predeceases you or cannot inherit for any reason.
3. **Work with an Attorney:**
   - Avoid generic templates and consult a professional to draft a trust tailored to your needs.

Mistake 5: Overlooking Digital Assets

In today's digital age, your estate likely includes online accounts, cryptocurrencies, and other digital assets. Failing to account for these can leave your trustee and beneficiaries without access.

How to Avoid This Mistake:

1. **Inventory Digital Assets:**

    o Create a list of digital accounts, including usernames, passwords, and access instructions.
2. **Include Digital Provisions:**

    o Specify in the trust how digital assets should be managed or distributed.
3. **Consider a Digital Executor:**

    o Appoint someone knowledgeable to handle digital assets and online accounts.

Mistake 6: Forgetting About Taxes

While revocable trusts offer many benefits, they are not inherently tax-saving tools. Overlooking tax implications can lead to unexpected liabilities for your estate or beneficiaries.

How to Avoid This Mistake:

1. **Incorporate Tax Strategies:**

    o Use the trust in conjunction with tax-saving tools like irrevocable trusts, gifting plans, or charitable donations.
2. **Plan for State Taxes:**

    o Be aware of state-specific estate or inheritance taxes that may apply to your assets.

3. **Consult a Tax Professional:**

    - Work with an accountant or estate planning attorney to develop a comprehensive tax strategy.

Mistake 7: Not Communicating Your Plan

Keeping your trust a secret can lead to confusion and disputes after your death. If beneficiaries are unaware of your intentions, they may question the validity of the trust or contest its terms.

How to Avoid This Mistake:

1. **Have Honest Conversations:**

    - Explain your estate plan to key beneficiaries and trustees to ensure everyone understands your wishes.

2. **Provide Copies:**

    - Consider giving your trustee and backup trustee a copy of the trust document for reference.

3. **Address Concerns Early:**

    - Resolve potential conflicts while you are alive to avoid disputes after your passing.

Mistake 8: Ignoring Legal Formalities

Failing to follow the proper legal steps when creating or funding your trust can render it invalid, leaving your assets unprotected.

How to Avoid This Mistake:

1. **Work with a Qualified Attorney:**

    o DIY estate planning may save money upfront but often leads to costly mistakes.

2. **Ensure Proper Execution:**

    o Follow state-specific requirements for signing and notarizing the trust document.

3. **Double-Check Ownership Transfers:**

    o Verify that all intended assets are correctly titled in the trust's name.

Mistake 9: Relying Solely on a Trust

While a revocable trust is a powerful tool, it should not replace other essential estate planning documents, such as a will or power of attorney.

How to Avoid This Mistake:

1. **Create a Pour-Over Will:**

    o A pour-over will ensures that any assets left outside the trust are transferred into it after your death.

2. **Add Powers of Attorney:**

    o Include financial and healthcare powers of attorney to manage non-trust assets and medical decisions during incapacity.

3. **Consider Comprehensive Planning:**

    o Work with an attorney to create a complete estate plan that includes trusts, wills, and other necessary documents.

Real-Life Example: Avoiding Pitfalls

Case 1: The Unfunded Trust

Steve created a revocable trust but failed to transfer his home into it. After his death, the home went through probate, negating the trust's primary purpose.

Lesson Learned: Properly funding the trust would have saved Steve's family time, money, and stress.

Case 2: Poor Trustee Choice

Jane named her oldest son as the trustee, unaware of his lack of financial experience. He mismanaged the trust's investments, reducing its value and creating tension with his siblings.

Lesson Learned: Choosing a professional trustee could have ensured competent and impartial management.

Key Takeaways

1. Funding your trust is essential for it to work as intended. Unfunded trusts leave assets vulnerable to probate.
2. Choose your trustee carefully to ensure your assets are managed responsibly and fairly.
3. Regularly update your trust to reflect changes in your family, finances, or the law.
4. Be specific and clear in your instructions to avoid misinterpretation or disputes.
5. Incorporate your trust into a comprehensive estate plan that includes wills, powers of attorney, and tax strategies.

By avoiding these common pitfalls, you can ensure that your trust fulfills its purpose—protecting your loved ones and preserving your legacy.

Chapter 13: Updating Your Revocable Trust: Keeping It Current with Life Changes

Creating a **revocable trust** is a significant step toward protecting your family's future, but the process doesn't end with signing the documents. Life is dynamic, and so are the circumstances that can affect your estate plan. Whether it's a change in family structure, finances, or the law, regularly reviewing and updating your trust is essential to ensure it continues to meet your needs and reflect your wishes.

In this chapter, we'll explore why and how to keep your trust current, common triggers for updates, and best practices for maintaining a robust estate plan over time.

The Importance of Regular Updates

A revocable trust is designed to be flexible, allowing you to amend or revoke it as your circumstances change. However, many people fail to take advantage of this feature, leaving their trusts outdated and ineffective.

Risks of an Outdated Trust:

1. **Unintended Beneficiaries:**

    - If you forget to update your trust after major life events, assets may go to unintended heirs.

2. **Overlooked Assets:**

    - New properties, accounts, or investments may not be included in the trust, subjecting them to probate.

3. **Tax Inefficiencies:**

    - Changes in tax laws can impact the effectiveness of your trust, potentially increasing your beneficiaries' tax burdens.

4. **Family Disputes:**

- Ambiguities or inconsistencies in your trust can lead to disagreements among heirs.

When to Update Your Trust

Certain life events and changes in circumstances should prompt a review of your revocable trust. Below are the most common triggers for an update:

1. Family Changes

- **Marriage or Divorce:**
    - Add a new spouse or remove an ex-spouse as a beneficiary or trustee.
- **Birth or Adoption of a Child:**
    - Include provisions for newly added family members.
- **Death of a Beneficiary or Trustee:**
    - Update the trust to remove deceased individuals and name new beneficiaries or trustees.

2. Significant Financial Changes

- **Acquiring New Assets:**
    - Ensure newly acquired properties, accounts, or investments are transferred to the trust.
- **Selling Assets:**
    - Remove assets from the trust that you no longer own.
- **Inheriting Wealth:**
    - Plan for tax implications and include inherited assets in your trust.

3. Relocation

- **Moving to a New State or Country:**
    - State laws governing trusts and estates vary. Review your trust to ensure it complies with local regulations.

4. Changes in Trustees or Beneficiaries

- **Trustee Resignation or Death:**
  - Appoint a new trustee or successor trustee.
- **Beneficiary Life Changes:**
  - Adjust distributions based on a beneficiary's financial stability, health, or personal circumstances.

5. Changes in Tax Laws

- **Estate Tax Thresholds:**
  - Federal and state estate tax exemptions can change, requiring updates to maximize tax savings.
- **Income Tax Rules:**
  - Modify trust provisions to account for new income tax implications.

6. Your Personal Wishes

- **Changing Goals or Priorities:**
  - Revisit your trust if your charitable giving goals, family relationships, or other priorities evolve.

How to Update Your Trust

Updating your revocable trust involves a formal process to ensure changes are legally enforceable.

Options for Updating Your Trust:

1. **Amendments:**
   - Use an amendment to make specific, minor changes, such as adding a new beneficiary or updating a trustee.
   - Ensure the amendment is signed and notarized, following state requirements.
2. **Restatements:**

- For significant changes, consider restating the trust. This process replaces the original trust document with a new version while keeping the original trust name and date.
- Restatements are ideal when there are multiple amendments or when you want to consolidate changes.

3. **Revoking and Creating a New Trust:**
   - In rare cases, it may be easier to revoke the old trust and create a new one. This is more common when major structural changes are needed.

Best Practices for Maintaining Your Trust

1. **Schedule Regular Reviews:**
   - Review your trust every 3–5 years or whenever a significant life event occurs.
2. **Work with Professionals:**
   - Consult an estate planning attorney to ensure changes are properly executed and compliant with current laws.
3. **Communicate with Stakeholders:**
   - Inform trustees and key beneficiaries about major updates to avoid surprises and confusion.
4. **Keep Records Organized:**
   - Maintain a copy of the updated trust and amendments in a secure but accessible location.
   - Provide copies to your trustee and backup trustee.
5. **Integrate with Other Documents:**
   - Ensure your trust aligns with other estate planning tools, such as wills, powers of attorney, and advance directives.

Real-Life Examples: The Need for Updates

Case 1: The Unintended Beneficiary

Karen created a trust naming her husband as the primary beneficiary and her sister as the contingent beneficiary. After divorcing her husband, Karen forgot to update her trust. Upon her death, her ex-husband received her entire estate, leaving her sister with nothing.

Lesson: Regularly review your trust after major life events to avoid unintended distributions.

Case 2: Overlooked Assets

Mike purchased a vacation home five years after creating his trust but never transferred the property into the trust. When Mike passed away, the home had to go through probate, delaying its transfer to his children and incurring additional legal fees.

Lesson: Keep your trust up to date by transferring newly acquired assets.

The Cost of Inaction

Failing to update your trust can create significant problems for your family, including:

1. **Legal Challenges:**
   - Outdated provisions may lead to disputes among beneficiaries or legal challenges from excluded parties.
2. **Financial Losses:**
   - Unfunded assets or inefficient tax strategies can reduce the value of your estate.
3. **Emotional Stress:**

- Ambiguities or errors in your trust can place an unnecessary burden on your loved ones during an already difficult time.

Key Takeaways

1. Life changes—such as family events, financial shifts, or legal updates—require regular reviews and updates to your trust.
2. Minor changes can be made through amendments, while significant updates may require restating the trust.
3. Work with professionals to ensure changes are legally valid and aligned with your overall estate plan.
4. Keeping your trust up to date minimizes legal risks, preserves your estate's value, and ensures your wishes are respected.

By committing to regular updates, you can adapt your trust to life's inevitable changes and maintain its effectiveness over time. A well-maintained trust is more than a legal document—it's a living plan that evolves alongside you, providing lasting protection for your family and legacy.

Chapter 14: The Role of a Trustee: Choosing the Right Person to Manage Your Trust

The **trustee** is the backbone of your revocable trust, responsible for managing its assets, fulfilling your instructions, and safeguarding your beneficiaries' interests. Choosing the right trustee is one of the most critical decisions you'll make in the estate planning process. An ideal trustee must possess financial acumen, organizational skills, and a strong sense of responsibility. However, making this decision isn't always straightforward, especially when family dynamics or complex estates are involved.

This chapter will guide you through understanding the role of a trustee, the qualities to look for, and strategies for selecting and supporting the best person (or entity) to manage your trust.

What Does a Trustee Do?

The trustee's role varies depending on whether the trust creator (you) is alive, incapacitated, or deceased. Regardless of the situation, the trustee is a fiduciary, meaning they are legally obligated to act in the best interests of the beneficiaries and follow the terms of the trust.

Trustee Responsibilities During Your Lifetime:

1. **Managing Assets:**
    - Ensure trust assets are maintained, such as overseeing investments, managing property, and paying expenses.
2. **Following Instructions:**
    - Carry out any specific directives outlined in the trust, such as disbursing funds for your benefit.
3. **Handling Incapacity:**
    - Step in as the successor trustee (if applicable) to manage assets and pay bills if you become incapacitated.

Trustee Responsibilities After Your Death:

1. **Distributing Assets:**
   - Ensure beneficiaries receive their inheritance according to the trust's terms.
2. **Paying Debts and Taxes:**
   - Use trust assets to settle any outstanding debts, taxes, or administrative costs.
3. **Continuing Trust Administration:**
   - Manage ongoing trusts for minor children, special needs beneficiaries, or others requiring long-term financial support.

Qualities of an Effective Trustee

Selecting the right trustee is essential to ensuring your trust is executed smoothly and without conflicts. Below are the key qualities to look for:

1. Integrity and Trustworthiness:

- The trustee must act in the best interests of the beneficiaries, avoiding conflicts of interest and personal biases.

2. Financial Competence:

- Managing investments, balancing accounts, and filing taxes require a strong understanding of financial principles.

3. Organizational Skills:

- Trustees must keep detailed records of all transactions and ensure that distributions align with the trust's terms.

4. Impartiality:

- For families with potential conflicts, an unbiased trustee is crucial to maintaining harmony among beneficiaries.

5. Availability and Commitment:

- Serving as a trustee can be time-consuming, especially for complex trusts. Choose someone who has the time and willingness to fulfill the role.

Types of Trustees

You have several options when selecting a trustee, each with its own advantages and disadvantages.

1. Individual Trustee

This is typically a family member, close friend, or trusted advisor.

Pros:

- Familiarity with family dynamics and your intentions.
- Lower cost compared to professional trustees.

Cons:

- Lack of expertise in managing large or complex estates.
- Potential for bias or conflicts of interest.
- Limited availability, especially if the individual has other responsibilities.

2. Professional Trustee

This includes banks, trust companies, or professional fiduciaries.

Pros:

- Expertise in managing trusts, investments, and legal compliance.
- Impartial administration, reducing the risk of disputes.
- Long-term availability for ongoing trusts.

Cons:

- Higher fees, typically charged as a percentage of the trust's assets.
- Lack of personal familiarity with family dynamics.

3. Co-Trustees

You can appoint two or more individuals or entities to serve as co-trustees, combining their strengths.

Pros:

- Balances personal knowledge with professional expertise.
- Provides checks and balances, reducing the risk of mismanagement.

Cons:

- Potential for disagreements between co-trustees.
- Slower decision-making due to the need for consensus.

How to Choose the Right Trustee

Step 1: Assess Your Trust's Complexity

- For simple trusts, such as those primarily holding cash or basic investments, a trusted family member may suffice.
- For complex trusts involving real estate, businesses, or tax strategies, a professional trustee may be more appropriate.

Step 2: Consider Family Dynamics

- If your beneficiaries have strained relationships, an impartial trustee can help avoid conflicts.
- Discuss your choice with family members to manage expectations and reduce surprises.

Step 3: Evaluate Potential Trustees' Qualifications

- Assess their financial and organizational skills, availability, and willingness to serve.

Step 4: Name Backup Trustees

- Always include at least one successor trustee in case the primary trustee is unable or unwilling to serve.

Supporting Your Trustee

To set your trustee up for success, provide them with the tools and information they need to fulfill their duties.

1. Provide Clear Instructions:

- Include detailed terms in the trust document about how assets should be managed and distributed.

2. Keep the Trust Updated:

- Regularly review and update the trust to ensure it reflects your current intentions.

3. Share Important Information:

- Provide the trustee with a list of assets, account details, and contact information for professionals, such as attorneys or financial advisors.

4. Communicate Your Choice:

- Discuss your decision with the trustee to confirm their willingness and understanding of their responsibilities.

Common Pitfalls When Choosing a Trustee

1. Choosing Based on Sentimentality:

- Picking a loved one purely out of loyalty may backfire if they lack the necessary skills or time.

2. Failing to Plan for Trustee Resignation or Death:

- Without a backup trustee, the court may need to appoint a replacement, delaying trust administration.

3. Overburdening a Single Trustee:

- Consider co-trustees or delegating certain tasks, such as hiring financial advisors, to avoid overwhelming the trustee.

Real-Life Examples

Case 1: Mismanagement by a Family Member

John named his eldest son, Tom, as trustee to manage a $2 million trust for his three children. However, Tom lacked financial expertise and failed to invest the assets prudently, reducing the trust's value over time and causing friction among siblings.

Lesson Learned: Select a trustee based on skills and experience, not family hierarchy.

Case 2: Professional Trustee Ensures Harmony

Sarah appointed a bank's trust department as the trustee for her blended family's trust. The professional trustee handled distributions impartially, reducing conflicts between Sarah's spouse and children from her first marriage.

Lesson Learned: A professional trustee can be invaluable for complex family situations.

Key Takeaways

1. The trustee is responsible for managing trust assets and ensuring your wishes are carried out.
2. Choose a trustee with integrity, financial expertise, and the ability to remain impartial.

3. Consider the complexity of your trust and family dynamics when selecting between individual and professional trustees.
4. Always name a backup trustee to ensure continuity.
5. Provide clear instructions and keep your trust updated to support the trustee in their role.

By selecting the right trustee and setting them up for success, you can ensure that your revocable trust operates smoothly and fulfills its intended purpose. This decision safeguards your assets, protects your beneficiaries, and preserves your legacy.

Chapter 15: Taking the First Step: How to Create a Revocable Trust Today

Creating a **revocable trust** is a proactive and empowering way to secure your family's financial future. While the process may seem daunting at first, it's a straightforward and manageable task when approached step by step. In this final chapter, we'll guide you through the process of establishing your trust, from choosing an attorney to funding the trust and maintaining it over time. By taking the first step today, you ensure that your loved ones are protected, your wishes are honored, and your legacy is preserved.

Step 1: Define Your Goals

Before you begin the process, take time to consider your estate planning objectives. Ask yourself:

1. **Who are my beneficiaries?**

    - Identify the individuals or organizations you want to inherit your assets.

2. **What are my priorities?**

    - Consider your specific goals, such as avoiding probate, protecting minor children, or supporting a charitable cause.

3. **Who will manage the trust?**

    - Decide who will serve as your trustee and successor trustee.

4. **What assets will I include?**

    - Make a preliminary list of the properties, accounts, and other assets you intend to transfer into the trust.

By clarifying your goals upfront, you'll be better prepared to make decisions during the trust creation process.

Step 2: Hire an Estate Planning Attorney

While it's possible to create a trust using online tools, working with an experienced estate planning attorney ensures that your trust is legally sound and tailored to your specific needs.

What to Look for in an Attorney:

1. **Experience:**

    - Choose an attorney specializing in trusts and estate planning.

2. **Knowledge of State Laws:**

    - Trust laws vary by state, so it's important to work with someone familiar with local regulations.

3. **Clear Communication:**

    - Look for an attorney who explains complex legal concepts in a way you can understand.

What to Expect During Your Consultation:

- **Discussion of Goals:** The attorney will ask about your family, finances, and estate planning objectives.
- **Explanation of Options:** They'll outline the different types of trusts and other tools that may be appropriate for your situation.
- **Fee Structure:** The attorney should provide a clear breakdown of their fees, which may be a flat rate or hourly rate.

Step 3: Draft the Trust Document

Once you've chosen an attorney, they will draft your trust document based on your instructions. This document serves as the legal framework for managing and distributing your assets.

Key Elements of the Trust Document:

1. **The Grantor:**

    - You, the creator of the trust.
2. **The Trustee:**

    - The person or entity responsible for managing the trust.
3. **The Beneficiaries:**

    - Those who will receive the trust's assets.
4. **Distribution Instructions:**

    - Specific guidelines for how and when assets will be distributed.
5. **Incapacity Provisions:**

    - Instructions for managing your assets if you become incapacitated.
6. **Successor Trustee:**

    - The person or entity who will take over as trustee if you are unable to serve.

Step 4: Fund the Trust

A trust is only effective if it's properly funded. This step involves transferring ownership of your assets into the trust or designating the trust as a beneficiary.

Assets to Include:

1. **Real Estate:**

    - Retitle properties in the name of the trust.
2. **Bank Accounts:**

    - Transfer checking, savings, and money market accounts to the trust.

3. **Investments:**

    o   Retitle brokerage accounts and transfer stocks or bonds.

4. **Personal Property:**

    o   List valuable items like jewelry, vehicles, or collectibles in the trust.

5. **Digital Assets:**

    o   Include cryptocurrencies, online accounts, and intellectual property.

6. **Life Insurance and Retirement Accounts:**

    o   Designate the trust as a beneficiary, if appropriate.

Step 5: Communicate Your Plan

While the terms of your trust remain private, it's a good idea to discuss your plan with key individuals, such as:

1. **Your Trustee and Successor Trustee:**

    o   Ensure they understand their responsibilities and are willing to serve.

2. **Your Beneficiaries:**

    o   Provide a general overview of your intentions to reduce the risk of misunderstandings or disputes.

3. **Your Family or Advisors:**

    o   Inform them of where your trust document is stored and who to contact in the event of your incapacity or death.

Step 6: Maintain and Update Your Trust

Life is constantly changing, and your trust should evolve accordingly.

When to Review Your Trust:

1. **Every 3–5 Years:**

    o   Periodic reviews ensure your trust remains relevant and effective.
2. **After Major Life Events:**

    o   Marriage, divorce, births, deaths, or significant financial changes may require updates.
3. **When Laws Change:**

    o   Tax laws and estate planning regulations can impact your trust, necessitating adjustments.

Common Mistakes to Avoid

1. **Procrastination:**

    o   Waiting too long to create a trust can leave your family unprotected in the event of an emergency.
2. **DIY Trusts:**

    o   While online templates may seem cost-effective, they often fail to account for state-specific laws or unique family circumstances.
3. **Failure to Fund the Trust:**

    o   An unfunded trust offers no protection. Ensure all intended assets are properly transferred.
4. **Not Naming a Backup Trustee:**

    o   Always designate a successor trustee to ensure continuity.

Real-Life Example: Starting Today for Peace of Mind

The Case of Lisa and Mark

Lisa and Mark, a married couple with two children, had been putting off creating a trust for years. When Lisa unexpectedly suffered a medical emergency, Mark was overwhelmed by the process of managing her finances and seeking court-appointed guardianship. After this ordeal, the couple created a revocable trust, naming Mark as the trustee and their adult daughter as the successor trustee. They also funded the trust with their home and savings accounts, ensuring their children would be cared for without court involvement in the future.

Lesson: Don't wait for a crisis to begin planning—taking the first step today can save your family from unnecessary stress and uncertainty.

Key Takeaways

1. Define your estate planning goals before creating your trust.
2. Work with an experienced estate planning attorney to ensure your trust is legally sound.
3. Properly fund your trust to make it effective.
4. Communicate your plan to key individuals to reduce confusion or disputes.
5. Regularly review and update your trust to reflect life's changes.

By creating a revocable trust today, you take control of your estate and provide your family with the security and stability they deserve. The process may require time and effort, but the peace of mind it delivers is priceless.

PLANNING YOUR REVOCABLE TRUST

Comprehensive Estate Planning Questionnaire

This detailed questionnaire is designed to gather all necessary information to prepare an effective estate plan, including Wills, Revocable Living Trusts, and other related documents. Please complete the sections thoroughly to ensure your wishes are accurately reflected.

SECTION 1: PERSONAL INFORMATION

1. **Full Name:**
2. **Date of Birth:**
3. **Social Security Number:**
4. **Current Address:**
5. **Phone Number(s):**
6. **Email Address:**
7. **Citizenship Status:**
8. **Marital Status:** (Single/Married/Divorced/Widowed)
   - If married, spouse's name and date of marriage:
   - If divorced, date of divorce and terms affecting estate plans (e.g., settlement agreement):
9. **Former Names (if any):**

SECTION 2: FAMILY INFORMATION

1. **Spouse's Full Name:**
2. **Children:**
   - Full Name, Date of Birth, Relationship (biological, adopted, stepchild), Address, and Contact Information.
3. **Are any children or family members with special needs?**
4. **Are any family members dependent on you financially?**
5. **Other Heirs or Beneficiaries:**

- Full Name, Relationship, Address, and Contact Information.

SECTION 3: HEALTH INFORMATION

1. **Do you have any health conditions that could impact your estate planning?**
2. **Do you wish to include provisions for long-term care or medical decision-making?**

SECTION 4: FINANCIAL INFORMATION

1. **Assets:**
   - Real Estate: Address, Type (residential, commercial), Ownership Structure, Approximate Value.
   - Bank Accounts: Institution, Account Type, Approximate Balance.
   - Investment Accounts: Institution, Account Type, Approximate Balance, Beneficiaries (if any).
   - Retirement Accounts (e.g., IRAs, 401(k)s): Institution, Account Type, Approximate Value, Beneficiaries.
   - Life Insurance Policies: Provider, Policy Number, Beneficiaries, Face Value.
   - Business Interests: Name, Type, Ownership Percentage, Estimated Value.
   - Other Assets (e.g., valuable collectibles, intellectual property, vehicles): Description and Estimated Value.
2. **Liabilities:**
   - Mortgages, Loans, Credit Card Debts, Other Liabilities.
3. **Income Sources:**
   - Employment, Pensions, Social Security, Rental Income, etc.

SECTION 5: ESTATE PLANNING DOCUMENTS

1. **Do you currently have any of the following?** (Provide copies if possible)
   - Will
   - Revocable Living Trust
   - Irrevocable Trust
   - Powers of Attorney (Healthcare and Financial)
   - Advanced Healthcare Directive/Living Will
   - Pre-Nuptial or Post-Nuptial Agreement
   - Life Insurance Trusts
   - Charitable Trusts
   - Any other estate planning documents.
2. **Have you named guardians for minor children?**
3. **Have you designated healthcare proxies?**

SECTION 6: DISTRIBUTION OF ESTATE

1. **Primary Beneficiaries:**
   - Full Name, Relationship, Specific Asset or Percentage of Estate.
2. **Contingent Beneficiaries:**
   - Full Name, Relationship, Specific Asset or Percentage of Estate.
3. **Specific Bequests:**
   - Description of Asset, Beneficiary's Name, and Relationship.
4. **Charitable Bequests:**
   - Charity Name, Address, Description of Gift.
5. **Do you wish to disinherit anyone?**
   - Full Name and Relationship.

SECTION 7: EXECUTORS, TRUSTEES, AND GUARDIANS

1. **Executor(s):**
   - Primary: Name, Relationship, Address, Contact Information.
   - Alternate: Name, Relationship, Address, Contact Information.
2. **Trustee(s):**
   - Primary: Name, Relationship, Address, Contact Information.

- Alternate: Name, Relationship, Address, Contact Information.
3. **Guardian(s) for Minor Children:**
    - Primary: Name, Relationship, Address, Contact Information.
    - Alternate: Name, Relationship, Address, Contact Information.

SECTION 8: TRUST PREFERENCES (if applicable)

1. **Purpose of Trust:**
    - Asset Management, Privacy, Minor Children, Special Needs, Charitable Giving, etc.
2. **Successor Trustees:**
    - Name, Relationship, Address, Contact Information.
3. **Distribution Preferences:**
    - Lump Sum, Staggered Payments, Lifetime Trust.
4. **Specific Instructions for Trustees:**

SECTION 9: SPECIAL INSTRUCTIONS

1. **Funeral and Burial Wishes:**
    - Burial, Cremation, Religious Ceremonies, Other Preferences.
2. **Digital Assets:**
    - Social Media, Cryptocurrency, Other Digital Property Access Instructions.
3. **Any Additional Wishes or Instructions?**

SECTION 10: ADDITIONAL INFORMATION

1. **Are there any potential disputes among family members to anticipate?**
2. **Have you considered tax implications for your estate?**
3. **Are there any other documents or issues not addressed in this questionnaire?**

Signature

I certify that the information provided above is accurate and complete to the best of my knowledge.

Signature: _____
  Date: _____

www.ingramcontent.com/pod-product-compliance
Lightning Source LLC
Chambersburg PA
CBHW071050240526
45469CB00006BD/2284